T0266012

# THE LOST MUSIC

KATRINA PORTEOUS

# THE
# Lost
# Music

BLOODAXE BOOKS

ISBN: 978 1 85224 380 7

First published 1996 by
Bloodaxe Books Ltd,
Eastburn,
South Park,
Hexham,
Northumberland NE46 1BS.

www.bloodaxebooks.com
For further information about Bloodaxe titles
please visit our website and join our mailing list
or write to the above address for a catalogue.

Supported using public funding by
ARTS COUNCIL
ENGLAND

Digital reprint of the 1996 Bloodaxe Books edition.

# ACKNOWLEDGEMENTS

'Ragwort' and 'Team Gut' were commissioned as part of 'Texts in the Landscape' by the National Garden Festival, Gateshead, 1990. 'The Blackbird and the Hawthorn' was commissioned by British Rail in association with The Public Art Development Trust for the National Garden Festival.

'Ragwort,' 'The Blackbird and the Hawthorn' and many of the poems in Part II were published in the *The Page* (*Northern Echo*, Northern Arts and Durham County Arts, Libraries and Museums).

'Team Gut' appeared in *Northern Poetry II* (Littlewood, 1991); 'If My Train Will Come' and 'Factory Girl' in *New Women Poets* (Bloodaxe, 1990), and *The Gregory Anthology* (Hutchinson, 1990); 'Factory Girl' was used in *The English Programme Handbook* (Thames Television, 1992-94).

'Astopovo' first appeared in *Landing On Clouds* by Olivia Fane, (Mandarin, 1994); 'Long Nanny Burn' in *Beadnell: A History in Photographs* (Northumberland County Library, 1990); 'Tree of Heaven' first appeared in *Trees Be Company* (Common Ground, 1989).

'Blackberries' and 'The Blizzard' were commissioned by Northern Electric for its magazine, *Northern Electric News* (1995). 'Inscription' first appeared in *Archaeology in Northumberland 1994-95* (Northumberland County Council 1995). 'Wrecked Creeves' appeared in *The Independent*.

Katrina Porteous would like to thank the Society of Authors for an Eric Gregory Award in 1989, Northern Arts for Writer's Awards in 1990 and 1992, and the Arts Council for a Writer's Bursary in 1993. All these made it possible to research and write the poems in Part II.

# CONTENTS

## I

## II

# I

*For P.Z.*

# The Blackbird and the Hawthorn

'Time is a globe,' said the blackbird,
Flitting with his airy views
Over the garden in which he sings:
'The past and present and future of things
All meet in the middle and fuse.'

'Aye,' said the hawthorn sadly,
'But we live by days, and die,
And though all is one at the heart, time's sphere
Looks flat as a railway track down here.
I can neither sing nor fly.'

## Factory Girl

Five nights a week I work as a factory girl.
My job's in Necklaces. Cartons of colourful beads
Run down the line and I thread them. The Sorter leads,
Popping them into their boxes – a difficult task,
For sometimes the green look blue, the blue look black,
And many fit all six boxes equally well;
But the Sorter has to be certain they don't get mixed.
Everything's made to fit. The order's fixed,
See, by the day, and we stick to it, or else
There's plenty others wanting jobs...

                                    My shift's eleven
At night till the early morning bell drills seven
Into my dreaming. Then I go home to bed.
I don't know whether it's dark or light out there.
In here it's always the same, summer or winter.
With all of our necklaces made to the book, as we thread
In the given order (green today, then red;
Tomorrow, red then green), to me they appear
So much the same; like the nights, the bus-ride here,
The sequence of stop after stop, long as the Tyne,
Counting the lights in the water, the broken line
Down where the shipyards were that went redundant.

I think of the oddest things to unsettle the pace:
Sometimes of Dad. I try to remember his face
And the stories my Mother told me: ('You should've seen
How he looked in his uniform, Hin, when he went to the War!
I don't think I'd ever loved him so much before.'
'What a knees-up we had when the fighting was over! At last
We were done with the sirens, the blackouts and rations. God willing,
He'd still have his job at Swan Hunters.' But that was gone.
'When he heard, he looked like a factory shutting down,
The lights going out in the workshops, one by one...').

Well, I string this together. I try to make sense of the past.
But pieces are all I have. I can't force them to mean
Anything much. I just see what I want to. It seems
A haphazard collection of memories, turned in the telling
This way or that by a whim, as an order's cast;
O, nothing seems to make logical sense any more.
I go home, and I dream of necklaces snapping, beads spilling
Into their moving millions, over the floor.

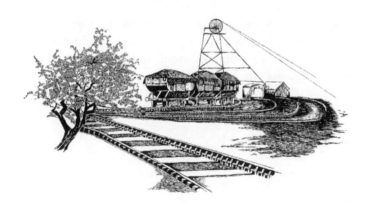

# Long Nanny Burn

*Beadnell Bay*

This place changes with every tide;
Buries the wheels and springs of World War II machines,
Twisting them deeper under the tons of sandhills
Like an obscene dream inside.

Down where the river scoops low, wind smooths, time passes,
Mounding the dunes up, carving them through from the floodland.
The sky, swept cold blue, sprawls enormously wide here.
Winged skeletons litter the sand.

But week by year, the river is shifting its wash.
It wrestles the irresistible push. The sea,
Its rage contained, inhales; retreats, revealing
Sharp-edged scrap, mud-sunk. Hard memory.

I've watched this, life-long, longer than all life; fighting
River, struggling, tight as a muscle, months; then suddenly strong,
Forcing its straight path through overnight, slicing the sand clean.
Nothing buried lies safe here for long.

# Astopovo
*The Countess Sophia Tolstoy Remembers Her Husband*


Lyovochka, as you waited in the station-master's shack
And all those cameras hovered round your bed to watch you go
Through the brimstone smoke and clatter of the railway track,
Eager for your shrivelled body, sheathed in linen, clean as snow,
Did you feel as if your family were huddled there around you
And curse their wretched babble, distracting you so,
As you did when you retreated with your writing to the orchard
When the children caught the measles? I was with you. Did you
      know?

Well, sometimes on a midnight when I heard you breathing by me
In the dark, after our wedding – is it fifty years since then? –
I would stroke your back and smell your sleeping body warm
      beside me,
Agonising how to make you let me know you, let me in.
A spelk in your finger, a sickness in your head,
I crippled you year by year; locked you up with shrieking children
Till you knew that you were going mad, slammed doors, and
      wished me dead.
Thus we grew slowly grey together, side by side, in bed.

When you left me in October as the orchard leaves were burning
I knew that all was over. Though I surely did undo you,
Lyovochka, just as surely as the trees will keep on turning
The salt earth into apples, I sustained you too; and truly
As you cursed the lust and dirt in us, hungry to be chastened,
Free in your work, as you bade me then goodbye,
You severed the thick roots that for fifty years have fastened
Deep into my heart and sucked it dry.

# Ragwort

Before this land was laid to waste
I fixed my will upon the place,
A weed of grass and open space.

When Midge Holm vanished – starved, deprived
Of soil – my new leaves sprang, alive,
From slag. I swore I would survive.

Under the black coal-blending tower
I split my buds and spat a shower
Of yellow sparks: a coke-works flower.

In Norwood Yard, where engines sprayed
Great downy plumes of dirty grey,
The wild wind tore my seeds away,

And where the stinking Team Gut swilled
Its tarry mouth out, I distilled
Bitterness in my leaves, until

My ragged kex stood winter-thin,
And shivered, waiting for the spring,
While all my futures slept within,

And all my memories, down below
The blue-black screenings, and the snow.
I loathed that blight, and loved it so.

Now roses blaze where men grew old
Burning coke and shovelling coal.
There's no ground left for me to hold.

Except beneath. I undermine.
My past and future intertwine.
Each spring, I rise. I bide my time.

## If My Train Will Come

If my train will come,
Quietly, in the night,
With no other sound than the slow
Creak of wheel upon wheel;
If, huge as a house but brighter,
Crouched at the edge of the fields
Like a steaming beast, it is waiting
Down the deserted road;
Though the colliery gate and the church
Where my mother and father were wed
Are all grown over at last
And the people I knew there dead now,
If a stranger alights
And, holding my breath, I see
That he has your eyes, your hair,
But does not remember me;
And if there follows a girl
With my face from years ago
And for miles by the sides of the tracks
The Durham grasses blow –
O, if my train will come
With its cargo of souls who have passed
Over this world to find me,
Will I go? Will I want to?

# Skylark

Suddenly above the fields you're pouring
Pure joy in a shower of bubbles,
Lacing the spring with the blue thread of summer.
You're the warmth of the sun in a song.

You're light spun to a fine filament;
Sun on a spider-thread –
That delicate.

You're the lift and balance the soul feels,
The terrible, tremulous, uncertain thrill of it –
You're all the music the heart needs,
Full of its sudden fall, silent fields.

# Calf

Outside my window a cow is giving birth.
Wrapped up in plastic, the calf dives feet-first
Onto the rain-sodden, trampled turf.

And at once it is desperate to be upright;
Heaves, flops, kicks as if sky was its birthright,
And not even the sudden slide from dark into daylight

Tugs like the gravity that drags it back to earth.

## Everything Must Fall

Yellow eats deeper into the green oak's leaves.
A woman pegging sheets out in her garden might recall
Softer days, now the wind knocks the roses
Hard against the wall.

They say there was never such a year for berries.
In the woods, brambles, bittersweet; in the fields, tall
Rowans and elders. Fruits hang by the handful.
Everything must fall.

Alone on the village bench, a girl rocks her baby
Under a sagging chestnut bough.
Summer has hardened her face. Last year's lovers
Know better now.

# Team Gut

*Who goes there?*  A scrap-yard river,
A brick-end, drowned-rat, rotten-wharfed river.

*Where are you heading?*  Into the future,
Jiggering out the wastes of labour.

*What do you carry?*  A shaft of nature,
Snaking its way through the neighbourhood factories.

*Who are your allies?*  The dark starlings
That blacken the sky like iron filings

Over smoke-stacks, gasometers, viaducts, tangles
Of rust-speckled dock leaves, and barbed-wire brambles.

*Filthy old gut, what plagues do you spread
Through these derelict works?*  I am memory's thread.

*How will you mend them?*  With hawthorn and rosehips
And fireweed, that burns and peels on the slag-heaps.

## II

*What do you remember?*
Far upstream,
Quiet fields of grass instead of factories,
Sedge turning green.

*What more do you remember?*
Before the Tyne took shape
I was a mighty river. Glaciers cracked me,
Grinding me deep.

*What else do you remember?*
Viking raids.
Men who arrived from nowhere, plundered, ruined,
Then sailed away.

*Is there more that you remember?*
Not long past,
Young lads mined my valley. Some were buried.
I remember dust.

*What more can you remember?*
Heat and flame,
The fire that buckles rock by the millennium; men
Who briefly did the same.

*What burned, do you remember?*
Bricks, glass, coke,
And pig-iron, white-hot from the furnace.
A cacophony of smoke.

*What's left, now, to remember?*
Poisons, the debt
Beneath the smooth, green lawns and tower-blocks.
People forget.

## III

*What does your name mean, River Team?*
To empty and give birth,
To mother, as water always has,
The billion-year-old earth.

*Then, River Team, what are men?*
No more than coal.
All life on earth is fuel for change.
Men are scarcely a moment old.

*But, River Team, what of their works —*
*Speech, society?*
As men forget, so each hurts each,
And all hurt me.

*And what is forgetting, River Team?*
Only the water
That colours all worn things thrown into it drab
As wormwood in winter.

*And what is remembering, River Team?*
No single water drop
That circles from sea, by cloud and land, to sea
Is ever lost.

And nothing that time or men can kill,
Or spoil, or change,
Is ever forgotten; for the stream
Of memory remains.

*Then what can you know of the grief of men*
*And women trapped in time?*
Only their bodies are water, mostly,
Moving, like mine.

## As Clay Remembers

As clay remembers
Beneath the shaping fingers
The shape it used to take;

As rope remembers
Its coil and, drying, twists, intractable
As snakes;

As seed remembers
After an ice-age of five thousand years
To wake;

As iron remembers,
Black and cold and beaten, where its weak point lies,
And breaks;

As the March wind
That tears through the streets like runaway horses
Remembers the mountains;

As the small rain,
darkening the pavement,
remembers the smell and colour of the endless sea;

As the night remembers
The order of drowned stars
Above the city;

As the day remembers,
Annealed in the heat of the furnace flame, erasing
World upon world, in waves,

Each day displacing
The last with no record of loss;
As tides effacing

The patterns of numberless sand-grains remember;
Or as a mother
Remembers the child inside, the child she was,

And, suddenly shaking,
Stops in her tracks and asks,
Are you gone for ever?

As the city sleeps,
As the rock beneath
Remembers every indelible line of its making:

So I remember
Love in my bones.

It is what won't be lost we keep on chasing.

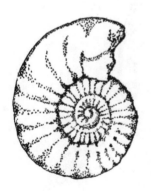

## Domestic

My knuckles ache to pin them down,
Fresh as they smell. White clouds stream whipstruck
Over the chimneys. In the yard
The loud washing cracks on the line.

They strain to be off, the sheets and socks
I've washed for them these seven years:
Shirts like sails and the kids' wild colours,
Safe, familiar ironing:

They fling themselves before the wind.
Barely a few pegs hold them back.

# The Clockmaker's Daughter

He is rapt in his world and won't leave it for anyone, certainly
Not for me.
He sits with the lens pressed close to his frowning eye
And never sees
How the sun from the skylight fingers each instrument,
Delicate, mutable.
He is making the final adjustments, he says, to a permanent
        measure of time.
It is beautiful.

There is softness, too, in the folds of his face, in the lines of his eyes
There is kindness; and yet
If you ask him the names of his late wife and children, he rubs his
        rough chin
And forgets,
And forgets, and goes back to his work; and I see to the order of
        things and am light,
Though, day by day,
I am filled with a terrible weight of unwinding, of sunshine
Slipping away.

Sometimes I dream I have stopped all the clocks; that the bottomless
Longing we feel
To be known, to be loved, is no more than the turning
Of wheel upon wheel;
And imagine his sadness then – nothing to do with the telling of time,
But the coiled fear in his heart, and the parcelling out of affection
Second by second: perpetual motion of wheels,
The pursuit of perfection.

# The Genie in the Bottle

You want to know what losing her is like?
Three years, and still I pace the room at night:
Want something to stroke. Want something to smother me.
Give in. Let go.
There's better loss in bottles. Whiskey? No.
The scent she used to wear.
Unwrap it slow.

O, I could travel down that scent for miles and miles.
Her skin, warm from the bath. Her hair. Her smile.
I'll breathe her in again. Those gentle hands,
Just here.
Drink down the deep green medicine
And she is near,

Just out of reach behind that half-shut door.
Yes. I can trace her voice, its shape and fall,
But not the words. Not quite. What do you say,
My sweet, immortal soul?
That there is more?

There may be. Come, lie on me. I'll confess.
It's weight I need. Your full length. I'll possess
The essence of you yet if you will come
And let me press
The perfume from you, squeeze you, shapely, soft
And yielding, breasts and neck.

Still nothing. Draw her deeper. What's enough?
A smile, perhaps? A kiss? A night, a life?
No one can know what losing her is like
Unless it be
To hold her simply, and imperfectly
Embrace what should be spirit. So
I set her free

And made a boundless scent of her, a lightness
That won't be caught or kept, or lost; can't fill
The space she's left in me. Love? It's an illness.
I'd have her still
If souls were pure as perfume. But there's more.
My fingers close round nothing where her soft neck throbbed before,
And I know it's not the genie in the bottle but the warm, unwieldy
        body
That I took my little knife
And spilled her for.

# In the Kitchen

Back turned to him, over the draining-board,
She sliced the quick knife down, again, again,
Let loose the bitter smack of orange rind.

He watched her. Was this all that she could say?
He wanted words. A strike. A spark. A flame.
And then – 'I didn't mean to be unkind...'

Instead, he took halved fruit in each big fist
And wrung the sticky juice from them, and licked
The sweetness from his fingertips, and wished
For hers. She hacked the rinds to matchsticks.

Her wrist flicked like a whip. He felt its sting,
Stirred sugar in the pot, and did not dare
Rattle the spoon, for fear of scraping her.

Above the blue and yellow flowers of gas,
The jam pan spat and spluttered, dangerous,
Filling the room with spicy steam, proving

That it is better to make marmalade
Than to talk about the taste of oranges.

# Comet Hyakutake

Midnight. The clouds are clearing. Overhead,
From the Dipper's upturned cup, a milky glow
Spills on the sky, due north; not sharp as the pin-prick
Stars, but a luminous, moon-white blur, like snow.

And if you stopped on the milk-bottle step to watch it
Unfurl its highway of light down the soundless sky,
Remote as the birth of the sun, the earth and the planets,
A mute, insensible envoy passing by,
Your heart would fly up, full of questions; but could not reach it,
For, like reflected light, in its reply
It throws the questions back: *Where are you going?*
*Out of which dark? Towards which dark? And why?*

# Tree of Heaven

Harvard has famous elms, Boston its maples,
Somerville, weeds.
Nothing thrives on the city's neglect like ailanthus.
It fattens, and breeds.
While oaks, beeches – Massachusetts natives –
Shrink back, poisoned by the Interstate,
Stinking ailanthus feeds
On the pear-drop scent of car body-shops,
The green oil-slick on the pavement:
Immigrant trees.

They are everywhere: at the roots of supermarkets;
They attack
Garbage skips, parking lots, doorways of seedy
Italian restaurants, creeping surreptitiously:
Buckle and crack
The backs of the sidewalks, bursting skywards
To glimpse the blue Boston roofline through the fumes.
On the rank railroad tracks
They stitch up the left-behind push-carts and milk-crates,
Undoing the past.

Soon bolted gable-high, they don't age well; their branches snap,
The cheap sticks split.
One strong wind can tear ailanthus' roots right out
And skittle it.
Seeding furtively behind the peeling porches, musty, dark
Back rooms of funeral homes and junk-shops, sloughing samaras,
They seem the opposite
Of a tree's true, permanent embodiment of place. And yet,
Though they're ephemeral, you can't get rid of them. They are
Wholly appropriate.

Ineradicable Heaven Tree: feather-leaves fanning
The stifling yard,
Where an old man sits cursing its stragglers that sap
The statue of Mary among his tomatoes,
It wheedles its hard
Suckers through shallow dust; drops hayfever flowers,
A litter of rusty keys; and nothing about it
Is lovely, apart
From its name and its green shoots, mending the damage
It springs from, like scars.

## Blackberries

*(for Jo)*


On the high iron railroad they drag their barbed wires
Through ditches, and twist
Up paths that look down over Consett, its fires gone out.
You are too young to remember.

But the sky is the colour of cold iron.
There is slag underfoot.
The hawthorn grows rusty. The dock rattles its seeds
Down the steep track. Each September,

Every year of our lives, Jo, we've climbed up here with buckets
Where the fat berries blacken on clinker.
The urge to pick them comes stronger than hunger.
Very soon, it says, it will be winter.

So fill your pails now for the time when there will be no blackberries.
Go home. Bottle them up,
Black as the midnight sky above the ironworks
Flaring red before the furnace doors clashed shut;

And over the sweet steam of the jam-pan, dream of December
And blackberries in February, and the shoots that already
Shove through the dust a gift from the dead to the living,
Older than words, Jo. As old as loving.

# Swallows at Nightfall

What is this cloud
Coming out of the south
Like a smudge of smoke, like a burning
Ravel of rope in the fading light?
Only the swallows
Returning,

Turning the pages
Of the year.
As sure as tides have reason
Inscribed in the migrating stars
And swallows
Have their season,

Here is a story told in grass
And sand.
Its random patterns
Harrow clouds
And plough the waves
And sift the whirling atoms

Until the world seems mad, unjust,
Unmeant.
And minute by minute
The sky is scratched
With grief and change.
And there is goodness in it.

As every story
Rights its wrongs,
The swallow strings stretch, swerving
Along invisible tracks that bring
A dark
Beyond deserving.

# I Envy the Cracked, Black Basalt

I envy the cracked, black basalt
Its incontrovertible form,
Fixed to resist the slow, sweet erosion
Of ocean and storm.

And the sea-swallow I envy for his lightness
And his leaving without the least look back,
And his pure, unmerciful, sky-high, ecstatic
Attack.

And I envy his roost, where the wind, tides and river
Contend to release
At last, from long battle, a landscape of absolute
Stillness, and peace.

And I envy the limpet his small, hard hold
Under wave after wave of blind water, his not letting go;
And I envy the sand,
That it slips through the cracks in the fastness of basalt,

And flows.

# Clouds

Let the tearing layers of dark and light
Be your lesson
In how you can want and not want
A thing to happen.

Far overhead, the high blue plain of the sky
Is scored by the plough
That claws the white cirrus in regular furrows
And carries it south

Impossibly slowly. Beneath,
The marbled planes of cumulus cloud
Drag east,
Rolling their shadows over the long fields.

If there is a time for the great question,
The Yes or the No
That sets the course of a life in relentless motion,
It is now

To the clouds you must turn in their endless becoming,
Winnowed and thinned,
Or filling to billow like white sheets. Choosing
Never ends.

For look. Above you, two vast ships with tense sails
Reach on the opposite tack,
Pulling apart and crossing each other's path
On the same wind.

## Dune Burial

Nothing was clear. I came out walking for some air.
Truth seemed
As many as the blades of grass the beetle
Hides between

And solid as the shadows on the sea.
The path had grown
Still steeper, when my foot trod in the earth
A ring of bone.

It was a human skull. I knelt and, touching
Gingerly,
Traced the faint chain of the spine, the fingers.
Suddenly

Summer had come to an end. The dry grass crackled.
Thistles hissed.
The sun was cold, and there was nothing left to say
But this:

*Kiss me. Kiss me again, and again kiss me.*
*Then tell me why*
*His bones curl so deep in the salty dust*
*And do not lie.*

# Inscription

*St Ebba's chapel ruins, Beadnell Point*

I am the boat
Hammered by wind and hard water
In whose hold rocked
The beautiful, the holy:
All wrecked.

Their bones sift in the sand.
What hands build,
Waves break
And the labours of bent grass and scurvy grass
Make and remake.

They are out of the sea's reach
And the sun cannot touch them.
Though wind
Tears seed from the thistle and snail deserts shell,
Summer or winter,

I am their harbour.
I am the water's edge,
The sea-battered boat and the light always burning,
A journey
And the end of a journey.

# The Lost Music

There is a place where it is all recorded.
Each look, each touch and kiss, each word, discarded
As casually as rain into the sea,
Is treasured there, and waits to be recovered.

The keeper of this place is known to you
From long ago. And yet he has no past

And makes no plan, and feels no weight of loss,
No fear, only moment by moment looses
A stream of random and beautiful
Notes without music.

Now, in the dark place, each of us forgotten,
We cry out for him to come down and save us.

Like the architects of buildings we shall not see,
The planners of gardens and the planters of trees
That will not be grown in our own children's lifetimes,
We beg him to tell us who we have been

In the world of light, and taste, and sunshine.
Let the broken moments receive their true names.

Come to us,
Singer of men's lives, make sense of us:
Play back the music we wrote without knowing.
Let us hear if it was lovely.

# II

*For Charlie*
*1909-95*

# Five Sea Songs

### I

Wund's freshenin', bonny lass –
Boats'll no be off the morn.
Aah'll bide abed aside on ee
An' hear ye breathe abeyn the storm.

Aa' peaceful like a bairn ee lie
Asleep, an' nivvor mind the roars
The seas mek mortal on the rocks,
The wund that rattles at wor door.

Aah'll nivvor kna what's in your hairt
Ma lass, sae true t' me, an' kind,
An' if God's good, ye'll nivvor kna
What blaa's the wetter white in mine.

### II

An' ma'n ye away noo, ma bonny, ma hinny,
Sae kittle, sae orly, tae foller yon harrin'?
*Aye, lass. Aah've the sair, sorry hairt on a hunter.*
*A boat needs an ocean as well as a harbour.*

God ga' ye fair wund, then, t' sarra your hunger,
An' may ye gan safe on the sea. Mind ee weel,
There's yen hairt at hyame wheere the wund canna harm ee;
A boat needs an anchor as well as a sail.

*abeyn:* above; *ma'n:* must; *kittle:* restless, itchy; *harrin':* herring; *sarra:* serve;
*yen:* one; *hairt:* heart; *hyame:* home.

42

## III

*Divvin't ee touch me, bonny lad.*
*Divvin't ee touch me, hinny.*
*If Fatther knew, he'd gan stone mad*
*T' see the divvil in ye.*

Come heor, ma lass. There is naen shame
That ever man can mind it;
This world's ower-full a grief an' pains
T' leave love wheor ye find it.

Tis no what folk'll say, ma dearie,
Keekin' roond thon doors.
There's stronger progs than feelin' feared;
Whae aye, an' higher laws.

As nature binds yon sea t' keep
Its limits an' no brek them,
When tide an' wund run fair, ma sweet,
What harm is't, then, t' tyek them?

## IV

A lonely life, lang hoors at sea.
Nowt t' think on
But hoo the years ha' flitten be',
His fatther gone
An' noo his mother bent an' grey,
An' him wi' naeone.

*keekin':* peeping, spying; *progs:* pricks; *be':* by.

43

Hoo mony winters sin' he forst come fast?
A fair few fled.
Varnigh as mony as Aah've stooden
In yon baitin' sheyd
Wi' pails a drippin' mushels
An' ma knife's bright blade
He's had me stowed in his hairt's howld –
An' nivvor sayed.

An' nivvor, whils' the salmon threshed
Atween his hands,
His broon airms starred wi' skyells, or whils'
His fing'er-ends
Bled at the heuks, his lips aa' skeyned wi' ice,
Did he let on.
No once. Aah nivvor wad a guessed.
A queer thing, yon.


V

It was no that he meant t' grow caa'd as the wund blaa's.
His kiss was no caa'd, nor his body telt lies.
But he once looked away, an' forgot what he come for.
He torned like the tide.

Yon's love for ee, hinny. It's dip as the ocean
An' light as the sunshine. T' hell wi' your man –
Some day he'll be nae mair t' ye than an aa'd stone
Happed ower wi' sand.

*mushels:* mussels; *howld:* hold; *skyells:* scales; *heuks:* hooks; *skeyned:* skinned;
*caa'd:* cold; *dip:* deep; *happed:* covered.

# The Blue Door

Beyond the blue door, everything is simple.
A century has dignified the clutter of tools
He cuts and saws and stitches with to a dusty likeness:
Old things are beautiful.

A blue light filters through the dirty windows
Where Charlie bores the creeve-wood with the brace and bit,
Its handle smoothed and seasoned by his father's fingers –
The perfect fit.

It has been a long day, and not an easy one;
The creeves sore-hammered, some to wrench apart,
Bow out of bull, and wrestle back to shape again
With labour, and art.

What seas have battered he makes sense of – slowly
Fingering twine to ash stick – like a story-teller. Duty
And memory are crosshatched on the face that bends to it.
If there is beauty,

Look for it in the telling of a story.
If there is meaning, seek it in the gloom inside
The blue door, where, like rope unravelling, the century
Is simplified.

*creeve:* crab or lobster pot; *bow:* curved frame of creeve; *bull:* supporting plank
in bottom of creeve.

# Charlie Douglas

'We're gan' tyek hor off, th' morn,'
Said Charlie, squatting in his black-tarred hut;
And the other old fishermen muttered, spat, swore.
So after a thin night, cracked by storm,
I arrived by the harbour kilns at dawn,
Where the sour *Jane Douglas* smoked and heaved,
Rocking her burden of dans and creeves.
And Charlie, a tab in his toothless jaw,
Stared blindly out to Featherblaa',
Tiller in hand. And away she roared,
Her proud bows rising, blue and white,
The same cold colours as the changing light
Bowling over the wind-torn sea.
Now, all the creatures that creep below,
Lobster and nancy, crab and frone,
From many million years ago
Have secret places, and Charlie knows
The banks and hollows of every part.
He's learnt their lineaments by heart
And mapped the landscape beneath the sea.
O, I was the blind man then, not he.
Now Charlie's quiet. His words were few:
'Aah'll tell ye somethin'. Now this is true –
We're finished, hinny. The fishin's deed.
Them greet, muckle traa'lers – it's nowt but greed.
Whae, there's nae bloody chance for the fish t' breed...
An' the lobsters! Y' bugger! In wor day
W' hoyed aa' th' berried hens away!'
'And they don't do that now?' 'Darsay noo!'
As he spoke, I watched the steeple grow
Smaller, still smaller, marking where
His folk, for the last three-hundred years,
Were christened and married and laid to rest.
So I urged him to tell me of all the past,
That other, hidden, deep-sea floor;

And whatever I'd cherished in life before –
Home, friends – just then, I loved him more,
This crined old man of eighty-two;
I wanted to trawl him through and through
For all the mysteries he knew
About the sea, about the years.
I wanted to haul his memories free
Like a string of creeves from the troubled sea,
Shining with swad and water-beads.
But turning his fierce, blind gaze on me,
His eyes said, 'Hinny, ye'll nivvor see –
Ye divvin't tell them aa' ye kna
Or aal your stories in a day.'

*dans:* marker buoys; *nancy:* squat lobster; *frone:* starfish; *berried hens:* female lobsters carrying eggs; *swad:* the green, fringed seaweed that clings to ropes.

# The Spelk

'Wha will keep the fires ga'n
When Charlie's deed? Man, every day
He's doon aback a the hut theer, saa'in'
The wood that borns the caa'd away.

'Aah should think he keeps ha'f the toon for' freezin';
An' as for the stories – divvin't ask!
When Charlie gets doon on his hands an' knees –
Whae, ye kna ye're away for the neet, ma lass!

'An' there's naebody knas hoo he stokes that fire
Inside'n the hut. When she's bornin' grand,
He tyeks a haa'd'n that mad-hot i-ron
Wi' his bayre hand!

'Noo he's getten a spelk! If ye'd hord him corsin'
As he hoyed them sticks he split aside...'
Here he sits on an upturned fishbox, nursing
His damaged hand: *'Ha' ye got good eyes?'*

Charlie, hinny, spreader of heat
And stories, sustaining the fires in Beadnell,
Says, *'Bugger, be sharp, mind! Dae it reet,*
*Or May'll fetch the bloody needle!'*

'Gi' us your hand, man, Charlie. Theer.
We'll tyek the point an' prog aboot –
By! What a spelk! Here – howk hor oot, man!
Howway, Charlie! Divvin't shoot, man!'

*spelk:* a splinter; *hoyed:* threw; *howk:* dig.

48

## Splicing Rope

'It's simple, hinny. Aal ye dae
Is born th' ends so th' divvin't fray,
Torn towards ye, an' push away.'
And the rope-ends knit in a seamless splice
As Charlie's bony fingers weave them.
And the hut walls creak. In the sandy bight
The seas rush in on the rocks, and cleave them.
It's come to a matter of touch, not sight,
In the years since Charlie's father taught him
With fingers brown as if barked with cutch:
'W' nivvor liked tarrin' ower-much.
Them hard bits stick in your hands, y' kna,
An' aa' the tar gits in, y' kna;
Ooh! Bloody morder, till it borst!
Naen painkillers then, y' kna.
Whae noo, th' canna dae nowt, y' kna,
Wi'oot them rubber gloves on forst!'
The hut is a safe boat, tight from the wind,
Warmed by the hot stove. Charlie's hand,
Safe on my shoulder, warm, weaves me
Tight with the boy on his father's knee,
Bound by the same yarns he spins me.
'Born th' ends so th' divvin't fray,
Torn towards ye, an' push away.'

cutch: bark used for preserving ropes and nets.

# The Blizzard

*6 February 1895*


*Why did they go?* Darse, th' ma'n no ha' telled
What was oot there yon morn', or they'd nivvor ha' sailed.

*It was quiet: what changed?* Come an aaful blaa'.
Wund for' the sooth-east. Seas. Snaw.

*Sudden?* Aye, was't! Like the crack 'n a gun
The sky torned black, an' the storm come.

Th' wore haalin' the lines, lad, eight mile oot
On the brattin' groond, in an open boat.

Wor Gran'fatther says, 'Cut away, boys! Torn
Hor heed t' the wund, an' fetch hor astarn.'

High as the castle, the seas broke. Forst
T' hit them swalleyed the two lang oars.

The second t' hit slacked aa' the nails.
Young Tom clung forra't, an' dropped the sail

For a dreg o' the wetter. Me fatther bailed,
An' Bill, poor bairn, he was lashed t' the mast,

For mony a time th' wore varnigh lossed.
Caa'd! Th' say, th' was that much frost,

Ye could brek the fish wi' your hands. Some storm!
Th' was two men drooned i' the mooth a the Born,

But wor boat – whae, it was aa' but night
When th' come t' the Langstone, snaw-blinnd, white –

Gan' ower the Knivestone, folk darsen't look...
*How were they saved, then? By skill? Or luck?*

Aye, hinny, hoo? Can ye be prepared
When it come like the wund, wi'oot a word?

She's like that, the sea. Mind, th' wore no feared,
Wi' their name on the boat, an' a strong hand t' steer 't;

Aye, an' somethin' higher than helm or hand.
They knew what it meant t' be a man.

The story of how many Beadnell and Seahouses boats were caught in the ter-
rible blizzard of 1895 remains a major emblem in local folk memory. Charlie's
grandfather, John Douglas, and his three sons, in their 21-foot coble the Jane
Douglas, were last to reach the Longstone.

*brattin' groond:* sandbank 7-8 miles off Beadnell, where bratt (turbot) netting
took place in summer and long-line fishing in winter; *dreg:* a sea-anchor, trailed
behind a boat to slow it down. *The Born:* North Sunderland Burn, Seahouses.
The coble Guiding Star of Seahouses was lost, John Walker and George
Dawson drowned. *Langstone:* Longstone Lighthouse on the Farne Islands,
where several boats took shelter overnight. *The Knivestone:* rocks on the north-
eastern approach to the Longstone.

# Benty's Swallow

They move to a different rhythm – wind, tide;
Answer to no one: a change in the light, an ear
Tuned to a breeze, to a memory – music the landsman
Can no longer hear.

Then out of the hut's dun recesses, the dark, sea-cured
Cavern of creeves, steeped rope, wood, rags,
Steps Benty; sniffs: 'She's comin'.' Stephen flings down
A blood-red flag.

Yes, she is coming, the spring, like Benty's swallow –
Colour, bustle, rows:
Freshen the paint on the coble. Nail on new plates.
Spread the nets. Stretch the tows.

And who can say what compels them? Even old Benty,
Sharp as the bird he watches for yearly, waking
To silence, lies still in the night and listens. 'Wund,'
He whispers. 'Sea's mekkin'.'

*tows:* ropes.

## All Changed

Last week the trees stood black and bare.
The door was shut against the wind
That dashed the birds and whipped the sand
And cracked the waves to blow like hair.

Three days, and that's all changed. The sea
Lies hushed and blue. The boats are down.
The nets are shot. The blackbird's found
The white hair of the apple tree.

# Spring Holiday

Inside, the hut is dim and smoky.
Deep shadows pull together
Brown tow and blue slowp and brick-red creeve-cover.
Dust changes everything to its own colour.

Bank Holiday Monday, and beautiful weather:
Out on the roadside, the buttercups dazzle.
The linnet begins his musical whistle.
Loud flocks of visitors migrate towards the harbour,

With no particular purpose in mind
And no idea
Of the faces like wood that watch them from the dark huts.
'Bloody good job th' wore no here,'

Stephen mutters. 'W' canna get wor nets shot
For aa' them bloody jet-skis an' speedboats gan' aboot.
What w' want noo is a foot a snaw t' fettle them.'
Down to the carpark rattle the rubber boats –

*Terminator, Sea Hog, Sea Devil, Gold-Digger*
Jostle one another, directionless, in the sunshine.
In the streets of Seahouses, children shout for ice-cream.
'Amusements,' flashes the sign.

'What th' come here for, onyway?' asks Charlie.
'Gan' aboot like bloody lost sheep.
Th' divvin't kna what work is. When we was youngsters
It was work an' sleep!'

Do they know? Can they say why they come? To stroll down to the
        harbour
With a vague sense that this is where it ends –
The land, the safe, the known. And they read the names there:
*The Guiding Light, the Radiant Way, the Children's Friend,*

And it all means nothing, like the huts' dark enclosure –
Too dense, too packed
With shadows; chains, tows, anchors, unintelligible voices
From the past.

'Whae, w' knew nowt else, did w'? What choice was th'?
The creeves, the lines – 'twas bloody slavery!' snaps Benty Jack.
'A bonny good job them days is gone an' aa', lad.
Ye want t' look forrard, no back.'

And he limps to the door, and looks out into the sunshine
At the stream of cars that speeds by unheeding;
And high on the hut's roof, the linnet is still singing
What spring means, and freedom.

*slowp:* fisherman's smock.

# The May Tops

This is what the tide casts back –
Shreds and scraps of Charlie's past.
Outside his hut lie sodden mats
Of slimy weed and leathery wrack.

They mend their creeves in the cluttered gloom;
Stitch and remember. Beside them, John,
Surly, irascible, whets his knife
On the curve of his grandfather's blackened stone.

'Aal alang the beach the now
Yon stinkin' wares, that's happed up broon,
What come ashore this time a th' eer,'
Says Charlie, hearing the waves bear down,

'Th' caal 'em the 'May Tops'. Aye. Aah've heerd
Th' aa'd men taa'k of it, right enough.
Oh, generations, they've kept that name.
The new growth pushes th' aa'd tops off,

Soon as the may come on the trees.'
'Divvin't believe a word he says!'
Sneers John, young bull-neck burning red.
'He's lossed his bloody wits wi' age!'

Darkly, Charlie looks away
Through the cobwebbed window, to the sea
And the shoreline, littered with shreds and scraps.
'Son, haa'd your bloody tongue!' he snaps.

*wares:* seaweed.

# The Harbinger

It tore down to earth. Bellowing like a dinosaur,
The rickety skeleton shuddered to rest on the water.
'An' Aah says, "Hey, Tom! Hey, Tom! Hey! – Lookee yonder!
A git muckle gate's come ower the Point!"' And it was Hawker.

*'O , let all hearts soar Heavenwards with the plucky young Airman
Who, on his Sopwith Waterplane, aims to be first to fly
Around Great Britain for our Nation's Glory,'*
The papers screamed: *'His Name Will Never Die...'*

August 1913: in Beadnell Haven,
History came to rest its engine. Charlie and Tom
Fetched water from the pump and went to bed by candlelight,
And had not heard of the Somme,

But slept at the tide's edge, and never dreamed of leaving.
Now, after eighty years, it would be harder to fly back
To where they stood than to the moon. 'We was just bairns, woman.'
They did not know what they were looking at.

*On 25 August 1913, when Charlie Douglas was four years old and Tom, his brother,
seven, Harry Hawker made an unexpected landing with his Sopwith sea-plane in
Beadnell Haven. His attempt to be the first to fly around Britain proved unsuccessful.*

# True Tides

'There's naen true tides,' snaps Charlie, 'on the beach, man.'
'Hoo's that?' asks Redford, teeming out fresh tea.
'Whae, Featherblaa's aal ebb, an' Robin Wood's Rock
Aa' flood.' These are old rivals at the sea.

'Noo, Charlie. Tell me this. I' Druridge Bay, lad,
Wi' lift on, mind – yon drivin' nets. Ye shoot,
Th' wesh ashore. Wor boat's nigh owertorruned.
But hey – yon beach nets – Charlie! Th' gan oot!

Ye hetti watch yon ootrogue. By, it's morder!'
'Damn, Reefor'! Bloody hell, man! I' wor Bay
Tide's comin' west until the Carrs is topped, man,
An' after that, she gans the tother way;

Ah, but she flows a couple hoors yet, man.
Yon tide gans east, an' still comes in. Hoo is't?
Top wetter pulls yen way, an' bottom tother.'
They strive against each other, clash, resist,

All afternoon over the scones. Then, slowly,
Look out to sea, cease arguing. Instead,
Each feels the tug of *yes* and *no*, and listens,
Certain something true has just been said.

*lift on:* rolling sea; *drivin' nets:* drift nets used for salmon fishing out at sea; *beach nets:* salmon nets anchored close to the shore; *ootrogue:* deceptive current pulling out to sea; *Carrs:* rocks in Beadnell Bay.

# The Sea Inside

Into a different element
We pull from the stony quay.
A chill wind breathes warm land away
And the uncertain sea,
Rippling light into darkness,
Dark into light, sets free
Rhythms that rock our boat and ropes
And shift us restlessly.

'There's nowt t' dae but wait, man.
There's nae fish.' Charlie scans
The empty miles. Why do I feel
Unsheltered, far from land?
Beyond, the Cheviot crouches,
Black Dunstanburgh withstands
The waves, the years; between them reach
The sea, the sky, the sand.

This is our forebears' country:
So the cold wind moans.
The stink of ware and salt on the fingers
And, in the bones,
The rush and heave of water,
Unknowable, unknown –
This is the sea inside us.
It rolls us round like stones.

# The Four O'Clock Alarm

*(Song)*

*Well, thank heaven that's the finish o' the four o' clock alarm;*
*Maybe now he'll have some money an' some time t' spend at hyame*
*An' the bairns'll see their fatther – him that barely knows their names –*
*Wor Bobby's left the sea; y' know, it's better that way.*

Whae, ye nivvor ha' the money for t' show them that ye care –
When the joiners' wives an' brickies' wives ha' money for t' spare,
Fitted kitchens, fancy bathrooms an' two holidays a year –
It's a wrench, like, for t' leave. She says it's better this way.

*We'll be just like other folk, now. He'll be workin' nine t' five.*
*Nae mair sittin' b' the wireless, wond'rin', 'Are ye still alive*
*Bobby?' – Dae th' never think oot there they've families an' they've wives?*
*Whae, wor Bobby's left the sea now, an' it's better that way.*

It's a queer thing tiv explain, like, why ye still want for t' gan,
When it's scarcely worth the diesel an' the fish is aa'ful thin,
An' it's blaa'n a gale a wetter an' the forecast says storm ten...
She wad nivvor understand. She says it's better this way.

*We wore married t' the fishin'. W' could never get away.*
*When the fish was thin he'd wait upon them thickenin' next day –*
*It's been sixteen year wi'oot a holiday.*
*Wor Bobby's left the sea, an' it's better that way.*

Ye can caa' yoursell a man, like; when ye gan oot a that door
Leave your hairt aside your sea-byates – ye'll be wantin' it nae mair –
For there's freedom on the wetter an' there's naen upon the shore
When ye're workin' for a wage. She says it's better that way.

*thin:* scarce; *thickenin':* becoming more plentiful; *sea-byates:* sea-boots.

# The Bottom o' the Sea

*(Song)*


Naebody knas the hoors w' put in, lads,
Barkin' an' tarrin' an' workin' on wi' creeves,
Wearin' oot w' women wi' mushels an' lines, lads;
Aah've gi'en ma life t' the bottom o' that sea, lads,
Aah've gi'en ma life t' the bottom o' that sea.

Noo we're dyen wi' the fishin' an' the fishin's dyen wi' us, lads –
Piercy an' Fiddler an' Jackie an' Ski,
An' aa'd Dick Haa', wha was drooned at the trootin' nets,
Quiet as a salmon on the bottom o' the sea, lads,
Quiet as a salmon on the bottom o' the sea.

Whae, naebody wants t' listen tae the fishermen.
Everybody tell ye what ye can dae an' ye cannot dae –
Haal a grand bag, then hoy the hyel lot owerboard,
Ploo'in' up the guts for' the bottom o' the sea, lads,
Ploo'in' up the guts for' the bottom o' the sea.

Jackie haa'd ma hand as he lay upon his deeth-bed;
'See ye i' the next life on the shores o' Galilee.'
Aah says, 'Ye'll no, 'cos Aah'll nivvor be a fisherman,
Or gi' ony thowt t' the bottom o' the sea, lad,
Or gi' ony thowt t' the bottom o' the sea.'


*barkin':* preserving ropes and nets; *dyen:* done.

## Decommissioning

They are burning a boat on the beach.
Grim-backed, they watch
In a darkness that crackles with fear.

Their faces leap up through the flames,
Masks hacked out of wood,
Reeling, red as blood,
Round the funeral pyre on the sand.

The planks sunder and peel
Like the great black ribs of a whale.
Unclenched, they fall,

And the sparks stream away on the wind,
And they sting like spray, smart
Like the ice-driven spray of winter
That burns in the dark –

An ache they would understand
And suffer more easily
Than the small white scrap of paper

Whose vacancy
Tells what the landsman knows
Of a boat and its burden.
Charlie, Jack, Stephen:

They slip away through the smoke,
So many nails wrenched free,
Unfastened from the sea.

# Longstone Light

Seven lang miles a' black wetter wesh atween
Yon light an' me.
See hoo she flashes an' fades in the hush
A' the dark an' the sea.

Aa' these night-fishin's lang a' the summer
Aah'm wonderin' why,
Wi' sic a smaa' thing as yon light in sae muckle a darkenin',
Aah can haa'd by hor?

Rock, ma boat. Tug at w' moorin's, wund, tide,
Aa' the black night.
There maun be a fair shoal a' ways for a man t' gan wrang i' this
          world
For ivery right.

# The Marks t' Gan By

I asked Charlie what a fisherman must know.
'Aal bloody things!' he answered me. 'How so?'
'A fisherman hetti hev brains, y' kna, one time;'
His fingers twisted round the slippery twine
In the stove's faint firelight. It was getting dark.
'Them days,' he said, 'w' hetti gan b' marks.

'Staggart, the Fairen Hoose; Hebron, Beadlin Trees...'
Thus he began the ancient litany
Of names, half-vanished, beautiful to hear:
'Ga'n roond the Point, keep Bamburgh Castle clear
The Black Rock, mind. Off Newton, steer until
Ye've Staggart level the Nick a the Broad Mill.'

Novice, I listened. In the gloom I saw
The rolled-up sail by the long-unopened door,
A traveller, stiff with rust, a woodwormed mast –
All the accumulation of the distant past.
'Now, keep the Chorch on Alexandra Hoose,
An' yon's the road...' 'Oh, Charlie, what's the use?'

I said. 'These memories! I know they're true,
And certainly they're beautiful. But how can you
Compete with all the science of these modern days?
The echosounder's finished your outdated ways.
Efficiency. That's what they want; not lore.
Why should the past concern us any more?'

I could not see his face. The stove had died.
'There's naen crabs noo,' said Charlie sadly, and he sighed,
And seeming not to hear me, sealed the knot.
'When ye see lippers comin', when t' stop
An' when t' gan – that's what ye need t' kna.
The sea's the boss. Me fatther told me so.

'Them marks,' he said; 'he handed aal them doon
Like right an' wrang. Them buggers for' the toons,' –
He sliced the twine he sewed with, savagely –
'Th' divvin't kna what's right. Th' gan t' sea –
Their only mind's for profit. They'll no give
Naen thowt t' hoo their sons'll hetti live.'

I saw, then. 'So,' I said, 'as we embark,
The past is map and measure, certain mark
To steer by in the cold, uncertain sea?
We leave it, like the land. But all we know –
What to hang on to and when to let go –
Leads from it…' 'Aye,' said Charlie. 'Sic an' so.'

*traveller:* iron ring attaching sail to mast; *lippers:* breaking waves.

# Wrecked Creeves

When I see lobster pots the sea has mangled,
The bow-sticks smashed like ribs, the covers tangled
Like wild hair round the lats, the strops all frayed,
It's not the wasting sea I think of, but the men who made them.

Whose hedge-knife stripped these ash sticks in the plantin?
His sea-boot bent each bow till, green and pliant,
Its arch sprang in his arms. Whose fingers, weaving
Strong knots, braided this net one firelit evening?

He hammered home the wedges, and his arm
Beat like a blacksmith's on the stubborn frame;
Deft, then, he intricately stitched inside
With a surgeon's delicacy and a master's eye.

Last week I found a plank stamped R.D.B.
He's dead. But Robbie's creeves still fish this sea
For other men, till east winds and spring tides
Return his broken sticks to the countryside.

There, on the live green grass above the beach,
They're strewn like human bones, worm-riddled, bleached;
And in the warm noon sunshine, bright with larks,
They say, 'Yon sea is caa'd, an' aa'ful dark.'

*lats:* cross-wise planks on pot's base; *strops:* ropes attached to pots; *plantin:*
plantation.

**Katrina Porteous** was born in Aberdeen, grew up in Co. Durham, and has lived on the Northumberland coast since 1987. She read History at Cambridge and afterwards studied in the USA on a Harkness Fellowship. Many of the poems in her first collection, *The Lost Music* (Bloodaxe Books, 1996), focus on the Northumbrian fishing community, about which Katrina has also written in prose in *The Bonny Fisher Lad* (The People's History, 2003). Katrina also writes in Northumbrian dialect, and has recorded her long poem, *The Wund an' the Wetter*, on CD with piper Chris Ormston (Iron Press, 1999). Her second full-length collection from Bloodaxe, *Two Countries* (2014), was shortlisted for the Portico Prize for Literature in 2015.

Katrina has been involved in many collaborations with other artists, including public art for Seaham, Co. Durham, with sculptor Michael Johnson, and two books with maritime artist James Dodds, *Longshore Drift* (Jardine Press, 2005) and *The Blue Lonnen* (Jardine Press, 2007). She often performs with musicians, including Chris Ormston, Alistair Anderson and Alexis Bennett. She is particularly known for her radio-poetry, much of it produced by Julian May. One of these poems, *Horse*, with electronic music by Peter Zinovieff, first performed at Sage Gateshead for the BBC Radio 3 Free Thinking Festival 2011, is published as an artists' book and CD, with prints by Olivia Lomenech Gill (Windmillsteads Books, 2014).

Katrina's third full-length collection, *Edge* (Bloodaxe Books, 2019), draws on three collaborations commissioned for performance in Life Science Centre Planetarium, Newcastle, between 2013 and 2016, with multi-channel electronic music by Peter Zinovieff: *Field*, *Sun* and *Edge*. *Sun* was part of NUSTEM's *Imagining the Sun* project for schools and the wider public (Northumbria University, 2016). *Edge*, a poem in four moons incorporating sounds collected from space missions, was broadcast as a *Poetry Please* Special on BBC Radio 4 in 2013.